D1262356

The Advent of Christ

Scripture Reflections to Prepare for Christmas

EDWARD SRI

SERVANT
BOOKS

PUBLISHED BY FRANCISCAN MEDIA
Cincinnati, Ohio

Scripture passages have been taken from the *Revised Standard Version*, Catholic edition. Copyright ©1946, 1952, 1971 by the Division of Christian Education of the National Council of Churches of Christ in the USA. Used by permission. All rights reserved. Quotes are taken from the English translation of the *Catechism of the Catholic Church* for the United States of America (indicated as *CCC*), 2nd ed. Copyright 1997 by United States Catholic Conference— Libreria Editrice Vaticana.

These reflections are based on Edward Sri, *Dawn of the Messiah: The Coming of Christ in Scripture* (Cincinnati: Servant, 2005). All rights reserved.

LIBRARY OF CONGRESS CATALOGING-IN-PUBLICATION DATA
Sri, Edward P.
The advent of Christ : scripture reflections to prepare for Christmas / Edward Sri.
pages cm
ISBN 978-1-61636-651-3 (pbk.)
1. Advent—Meditations. 2. Christmas—Meditations. 3. Jesus Christ—Nativity—Meditations. 4. Sri, Edward P. Dawn of the Messiah. I. Title.
BV40.S65 2013
242'.33—dc23
2013011932

ISBN 978-1-61636-651-3
Copyright ©2013, Edward Sri. All rights reserved.

Published by Servant Books, an imprint of Franciscan Media.
28 W. Liberty St.
Cincinnati, OH 45202
www.FranciscanMedia.org

Printed in the United States of America.
Printed on acid-free paper.
13 14 15 16 17 5 4 3 2 1

To my son, Luke.

CONTENTS

INTRODUCTION

Perhaps the Christmas story has become almost *too* familiar.

Every December we encounter the story of Christ's birth in manger scenes, Christmas cards, and decorations on Christmas trees. We hear it in Scripture, sing it in carols, and see it in the paintings, statues, and stained-glass windows that decorate our churches. For many today, the basic outline of the narrative has become so familiar that the profound—indeed, shocking—nature of the Christmas mystery might be overlooked. A virgin giving birth, a child laid in a manger, and shepherds greeted by angels no longer arrest our attention.

But what if we had never heard the story before? What if we were Jews in the first century who were hearing this plot for the first time? These events at the dawn of Christianity certainly would not be taken for granted. They would signal that everything our people had been longing for—for hundreds of years—was now coming to fulfillment.

This Advent I invite you to put yourself in that first-century Jewish world and discover the spiritual treasures that are packed into practically every line and every detail of the Gospel accounts of Matthew and Luke (the two Gospels that provide the narratives about Jesus's birth). Using excerpts from my book *Dawn of the Messiah*, the following material bridges the gap between unfamiliar ancient Jewish themes and traditions and our contemporary understanding of familiar biblical stories. My prayer is that this Advent experience will give you new perspective about the dawn of the Messiah—the Advent of Christ!

WEEK ONE

Setting the Stage: The Prophecies and the Hope

It has been said that Luke begins his Gospel like a good Shakespearean play: with a pair of minor characters who prepare the way for the lead roles to take the stage. Before the main drama surrounding Joseph, Mary, and Jesus begins, the first scene in the Gospel of Luke introduces us to an important supporting cast: Zechariah and Elizabeth, an older Jewish couple who are about to be caught up into God's plan of salvation in a way they probably never imagined.

Zechariah and Elizabeth stand out as a couple with high credentials in first-century Judaism. With Zechariah serving as a priest, and his wife also coming from the priestly family of Aaron, they would hold a position of great respect. Luke, furthermore, goes out of his way to emphasize that they are both "righteous before God" and even "blameless" in following all God's commands.

That is why the next statement would be so shocking to Jewish minds: "But they had no child, because Elizabeth was barren, and both were advanced in years" (Luke 1:7). Barrenness was often considered shameful in Judaism. It was even seen in some cases as evidence of God's punishment (see Deuteronomy 28:15, 18). So this statement introduces us to a tension between this couple's holiness on one hand and their childlessness on the other. Elizabeth waits for God to act in her life. And the reader of Luke's Gospel also waits to see how this tension will be resolved.

The Gospel of Matthew starts in a very different way. Matthew begins the story of Jesus with a long genealogy. It seems like the dullest of introductions: a list of forty-seven names. But for the Jews living in the first century, each name told a story and recalled important places, events, and periods in Israel's history. As we journey through this genealogical summary of Israel's history, we will see how Matthew strategically shows that God's plan for Israel is reaching its climax.

During this first week of Advent, the stage is being set for the greatest drama of all time.

SUNDAY | *The New Elijah*

> But the angel said to him, "Do not be afraid, Zechariah, for
> your prayer is heard, and your wife Elizabeth will bear you
> a son, and you shall call his name John.
> And you will have joy and gladness,
> and many will rejoice at his birth."
>
> —Luke 1:13–14

What is most interesting about this scene is not simply that
Zechariah and Elizabeth finally will be blessed with a child. This
child will bring blessings not only to his parents but to all of the
people, for John the Baptist will be one of the most important
prophets ever sent to Israel. Let us consider three amazing things
the angel tells Zechariah about this child.

First, he will not consume wine or strong drink (v. 15). In the Old
Testament, "Nazirites" consecrated themselves to God by a vow
and separated themselves from normal life. Abstaining from alcohol
was a common practice for the Nazirites (see Numbers 6:3; Judges
13:4). So this fact about John the Baptist indicates that he will be set
apart for some special service for the Lord, like a Nazirite.

Second, the angel's description of the child's being "filled with
the Holy Spirit, even from his mother's womb" (v. 15) tells us about
the kind of service for which John is destined: He will be *a prophet*.
It was the Spirit descending on Saul who transformed him into
a prophet (see 1 Samuel 10:10), and it was the Spirit of the Lord

who spoke through David so that God's Word would be upon his tongue (see 2 Samuel 23:2). It was this same Spirit who came upon the prophets Ezekiel, Elijah, and Elisha during their ministry in Israel (see Ezekiel 11:5; 2 Kings 2:9–16; see also Joel 2:28). The child "being filled with the Holy Spirit" indicates that John, too, will be a prophet.

Third, the importance of John's prophetic ministry is seen in the final words that the angel uses to describe this child:

> He will go before him in the spirit and power of Elijah,
> to turn the hearts of the fathers to the children,
> and the disobedient to the wisdom of the just,
> to make ready for the Lord a people prepared. (Luke 1:16–17)

These verses echo the last prophetic words of the Old Testament, where Malachi announces that the Lord one day would come to redeem Israel and that he would send his messenger to prepare the people for his arrival (see Malachi 3:1), and this messenger would be like a new Elijah: "Behold, I will send you Elijah the prophet... and he will turn the hearts of fathers to their children and the hearts of children to their fathers (Malachi 4:5–6). In light of this Old Testament background, the angel describes John's ministry as the fulfillment of Malachi's prophecy—he will be the new Elijah, preparing the people of Israel for the Lord's coming, which will bring about the reconciliation of families to God and families to each other.

And so, this story is not simply about God's intervening to bless a pious Jewish couple with a child. Rather, *the story is representative of the story of Israel.* Just as Zechariah and Elizabeth are barren and hope for God to show favor by blessing them with a child, so, too, the Jews suffer and long for God to show them favor again by visiting his people. God will respond to Zechariah and Elizabeth's desires for a child in a way that answers the needs of *all* the Jewish people: by sending them a son who will prepare the way for the coming of the Lord and the restoration of Israel.

FOR REFLECTION

What are some things I can do each day this Advent to prepare spiritually for Christmas?

> *Dear Lord, I pray that I will not take Christ's birth for granted. In these four weeks of Advent, prepare my heart for your coming this Christmas.*

MONDAY | *"I Am Gabriel"*

> And Zechariah said to the angel, "How shall I know this?
> For I am an old man, and my wife is advanced in years."
> And the angel answered him, "I am Gabriel, who stand in
> the presence of God; and I was sent to speak to you, and to
> bring you this good news."
>
> —Luke 1:18–19

Zechariah's question seems reasonable enough to us. But the angel gives a mystifying response: "I am Gabriel." Zechariah did not ask for the angel's name; he asked for assurances!

Imagine meeting someone on an airplane who advises you to buy many lottery tickets because you are going to win the lottery sometime this year. Wondering why you should trust this stranger's advice, you ask him, "How can I believe this will really happen?" What would you think if the man answered your question simply by giving you his name? "I'm Mr. Smith": How would *that* answer your question?

Yet the angel Gabriel knew what he was doing. He gave Zechariah the one bit of information that might help him tie all the pieces together. This one detail might help Zechariah see that God was really acting in his very own family's life in order to bring the story of Israel to its climactic turning point.

Revealing his name was significant because the only time Gabriel is mentioned in the Old Testament is in the important visions given to the prophet Daniel. In Daniel 9 the prophet was praying for God to show mercy on his people and bring an end to the Jewish sufferings under foreign oppressors. In the middle of Daniel's prayer, the angel Gabriel appeared to him at the hour of the evening sacrifice—the time when the incense would have been offered in the temple.

Gabriel delivered a message of good news and bad news to Daniel. On one hand, the people would continue to suffer under pagan nations for a long time to come. On the other hand, at the end of this period of suffering, God would send an anointed prince (the Messiah) to bring an end to sin and atone for iniquity. This anointed one would usher in everlasting righteousness and bring all of Israel's prophecies to fulfillment (see Daniel 9:24–27).

We can see that Gabriel is no ordinary angel. Revealing his name recalls the prophecies of Daniel 9. The parallels between what happened to Daniel and what just happened to Zechariah highlight this connection even more: Like Daniel, Zechariah *prays on behalf of Israel* as he offers the incense in the temple (see Luke 1:9). Like Daniel, Zechariah makes this prayer *at the hour of the temple sacrifice* (see Luke 1:10). And in the middle of Zechariah's liturgical service, the same angel—*Gabriel*—appears (see Luke 1:11, 19). Luke is clearly inviting his readers to hear the harmony in salvation history and view Zechariah's encounter with the angel in correspondence with Daniel's.

So, Gabriel is revealing a lot more than his name. He is subtly announcing that Daniel 9 is finally coming to fulfillment, and

Zechariah's own son is going to play a key part in preparing the people for the long-awaited "anointed one"—the one Gabriel himself originally said would atone for sin, bring everlasting righteousness, and fulfill all prophecy!

FOR REFLECTION

How do I respond when God answers prayer in ways I don't expect?

Dear God, as Gabriel did with Zechariah, often you answer my questions with answers I don't fully understand. But I trust you and your purposes. During this Advent season, help me see your larger picture for my life.

TUESDAY | *Great Beginnings*

> The book of the genealogy of Jesus Christ, the son of
> David, the son of Abraham.
>
> —Matthew 1:1

Matthew's first words bring us all the way back to the beginning of the Bible, the book of Genesis. Matthew 1:1 can be translated literally, "*The book of the genesis* of Jesus Christ." This is significant because similar expressions were used in Genesis to announce great beginnings.

For example, a similar formula was used to sum up the story of how God created the universe: "These are the generations of the heavens and the earth when they were created" (Genesis 2:4). This formula also was used to introduce the family tree of our first parents, Adam and Eve: "the book of the generations of Adam" (Genesis 5:1). In Genesis 10:1, the same phrase introduces the genealogy of Noah's family—the new human family who survived after the flood.

In each of these cases—Adam and creation, Noah and the flood—the phrase "the book of the genealogy" signals a significant starting point in God's plan for humanity. By opening his Gospel with these words, Matthew announces that another new beginning is here. The child at the end of this genealogy will bring about a new genesis: the renewal of all humanity and the restoration of the entire created order to harmony with God.

FOR REFLECTION

What new thing does God want to do in my life during these weeks of Advent?

Dear Jesus, prepare my heart to welcome you. Open my eyes to recognize that you will be born anew in me, and show me how to make room for you!

WEDNESDAY | *Worldwide Blessing*

Jesus Christ…the son of Abraham.

—Matthew 1:1

We dwell on this first verse of Matthew's genealogy to consider the description of Jesus as "the son of Abraham." For an ancient Israelite, such a description meant a lot more than being a physical descendant of this great patriarch. Being a son of Abraham is at the very heart of Israelite national identity.

God promised Abraham that his descendants one day would become a great *nation* (see Genesis 12:2; see also 15:18) and that *kings* eventually would come forth from Abraham's line (Genesis 17:6, 16). Jews in the first century would have seen that these two promises already were fulfilled when Israel became a *nation* in the time of Moses and a *kingdom* in the time of David.

However, there was one promise made to Abraham that had yet to be fulfilled, and it was the greatest promise of all. In response to Abraham's faithfulness, God swore that Abraham's descendants eventually would serve as *an instrument to bring blessing to all the peoples of the world:* "And by your descendants shall all the nations of the earth bless themselves, because you have obeyed my voice" (Genesis 22:18). This third promise gave rise to the Jewish belief that, one day, people from all the pagan nations would come to worship the one true God and be united with Israel in one covenant family.

By tracing Jesus's lineage specifically to Abraham, Matthew is drawing our attention to this worldwide mission of Israel. And such an allusion might stir hope that the child at the end of the genealogy will be the one to fulfill the long-awaited third promise and bring blessing to the entire human family.

FOR REFLECTION

How might I become an instrument for God to extend his blessing to others in the world?

God, sometimes I get so caught up in my own life that I become blind to the needs of those around me. Open my eyes this Advent to see how my life fits into the larger story of your plan for the human family.

THURSDAY | *Son of David*

Jesse [was] the father of David the king.
And David was the father of Solomon.

—Matthew 1:6

Our journey through Jesus's genealogy now brings us to the great king, David. A first-century Jew reading about "David the king" and his son Solomon certainly would recall the glory days of the kingdom of Israel. These men were the royal heroes of old who brought Israel to its greatest moment in history. In the time of David and Solomon, three important symbols of Israel's national identity—the land, the king, and the temple—shined most brightly.

First, the Promised Land was like a new Eden, the home for the covenant family of God. It was the place where the Lord would bestow blessings on his people and one day regather the pagan nations to himself. This sacred Promised Land was secured for Israel under the leadership of David and Solomon. Second, the kingdom was based on a covenant God made with David's family, and it had a universal scope. God promised an everlasting dynasty that would extend to the ends of the earth. This dynasty was founded on King David and his son Solomon. Third, the temple in Jerusalem was not just a place of worship; the Jews believed that the one true God who created the entire cosmos dwelt in a unique way with the Jewish people in this sacred spot. David envisioned the need for the temple of the Lord, and Solomon built it in Jerusalem. So when a first-century Jew would read about David and Solomon, this would bring to mind the highest point in Israel's history—the times when Israel had the land, had a king, and had God dwelling among them in the temple.

FOR REFLECTION

What "glory days" in my life can I remember? How have they shaped me and my faith?

Dear Jesus, thank you for the moments when, like Israel under David and Solomon, I have experienced the blessings of your reign in my life and an awareness of your presence in my heart.

FRIDAY | *Hope of the Nation*

> Josiah [was] the father of Jechoniah and his brothers, at the
> time of the deportation to Babylon.
>
> —Matthew 1:11

Now we come to the most somber note in Jesus's genealogy, recalling the tragic events of 586 B.C. Matthew does not mention "the time of deportation to Babylon" simply as a chronological marker. Rather, this verse brings to mind all that the Jews lost when Babylon invaded Jerusalem and carried the people away into exile. This was the moment when Israel lost the three great symbols of their national identity: the land, the king, and the temple. Babylon took over the land, destroyed the temple, and carried the king and his people away into exile in Babylon.

Israel was still suffering the consequences of this tragedy at the time of Jesus's birth. The Jews still did not have control over their land. They still did not have a son of David to rule them. And they still were longing for God's presence to be with them again in the temple.

Nevertheless, God offered the Jewish people hope in the midst of their sufferings. Through the prophets he announced that one day he would send a new royal descendant of David, a new anointed king called "the Messiah" (meaning "anointed one"). This Messiah-King would usher in a new era in which the Jews would regain the land, the kingdom would be restored to its former glory, and God's presence would return to Israel.

Matthew's Gospel calls upon those hopes when it introduces a man named Zerubbabel, who stands as a turning point in the genealogy:

> And after the deportation to Babylon: Jechoniah was the father of Shealtiel, and Shealtiel the father of Zerubbabel, and Zerubbabel the father of Abiud, and Abiud the father of Eliakim, and Eliakim the father of Azor, and Azor the father of Zadok, and Zadok the father of Achim, and Achim the father of Eliud, and Eliud the father of Eleazar, and Eleazar the father of Matthan, and Matthan the father of Jacob, and Jacob the father of Joseph. (Matthew 1:12–16)

As one of the leaders in the rebuilding of Jerusalem in 515 B.C., Zerubbabel represents the last Davidic descendant in Matthew's genealogy for which there is any public record in the Jewish Scriptures (see the book of Ezra). What happened to the sons of David from this period all the way up to the time of Jesus remained somewhat of a mystery.

This is what would make verses 13 through 16 so exciting to the original hearers of Matthew's Gospel: The royal line has continued for many generations after Zerubbabel! With each new name—Abiud, Eliakim, Azor, and so on—Matthew's genealogy introduces another Davidic descendant previously unknown in the Hebrew Scriptures. The genealogy thus picks up momentum in these verses, building hope that at the end of this family tree we might find that ultimate son of David whom the prophets foretold would return Israel to its former glory.

FOR REFLECTION

Are there areas in my life where I am "exiled from God"? How can I return to him?

God, sometimes I get so focused on the troubles in my life—at work, with my family, in my relationships—that I can almost forget the deepest problem you want to address in me: my sin. Help me this Advent to return to you and be liberated more from my sins.

SATURDAY | *The Return of the King*

> Jacob [was] the father of Joseph the husband of Mary, of
> whom Jesus was born, who is called Christ.
>
> —Matthew 1:16

Finally the genealogy's rushing crescendo reaches its peak. Here the royal line culminates with the child who will bring Israel's history to its ultimate destination.

The significance of this child can be seen in the three titles he receives in this opening chapter of Matthew's Gospel: Jesus, Christ, and Emmanuel (see Matthew 1:23). Perhaps one could see in these three names hope that the three Jewish symbols that were shattered in the exile now would be restored: the land, the king, and God's presence in the temple.

First, in Hebrew the name *Jesus* means "God saves." And Matthew highlights the specific reason for which the child is given this name: "He will save his people from their sins" (1:21). This is significant because, according to the Jewish Scriptures, it was Israel's sin that led to its losing the Promised Land. Sin led to the exile. Hence the deepest problem that Israel faced was not exile from the land but exile from God. This child Jesus has come primarily to save Israel not from the Roman forces occupying their land, but from the much deeper oppression of sin.

It is also significant that the child's name, Jesus, is a shortened form of the name Joshua. This might recall the famous Old Testament

Joshua, Moses's successor, who brought the Exodus story to its climax by guiding the people into the Promised Land. Just as the Joshua of old led Israel out of the desert wilderness and into the land, so now Jesus—the new Joshua—will lead the people out of their spiritual exile from God and into the true Promised Land of heaven.

Second, Jesus is given the royal title "Christ" (1:16). In the New Testament, the Greek word *christos* was commonly used as a translation of the Hebrew word *messiah* ("anointed one"). This was the title for the future son of David, whom the prophets said would restore the dynasty and bring to fulfillment the promises about a worldwide, everlasting kingdom. Matthew's genealogy joyfully proclaims that Jesus is that Messiah-King—the first Davidic Son to reign in over five centuries and the one who will restore the kingdom to Israel.

Finally, perhaps the most profound title given to Jesus comes at the end of Matthew's opening chapter. In Matthew 1:23, Jesus is called "Emmanuel," which means "God with us."

God's visible presence had not dwelt in the temple for more than five hundred years. Without a king, without control of their land, and especially without the glory of the Lord dwelling among them, the Jews in the first century might have felt somewhat abandoned. Many would have been wondering what had happened to God's commitment to Israel and all the great promises he had made to their ancestors. They certainly would have been longing for God to be with them again.

In the midst of this uncertainty, Matthew announces that the child at the end of this genealogy is "Emmanuel, which means God with us." In other words, God is with his people again! What is most astonishing, however, is that God is with his people as never before. In ages past God manifested his presence in the form of a cloud in the temple. Now the God of the universe actually dwells among them in the person of Jesus Christ.

FOR REFLECTION

How do I know God is with me today?

Jesus Christ, Emmanuel, thank you for coming into this world. Help me this Advent to be more aware of your presence in my life each day.

WEEK TWO

Serving God's Plan: St. Joseph, Zechariah, and John the Baptist

This week we continue our look at some of the humble persons who played significant roles in the coming of Jesus.

The new man on the scene is St. Joseph. In all the New Testament, he has no lines and few dramatic actions. Luke's Gospel simply portrays him as betrothed to Mary, coming from the royal line of David, and living in the insignificant village of Nazareth. In Matthew's Gospel, Joseph is "the husband of Mary" and the foster father of Jesus, serving as the guardian of the Holy Family. He transports his wife and child from Bethlehem to Egypt in order to avoid Herod's plot to kill the Christ child. Then Joseph leads his family back to Nazareth when the murderous threat has subsided.

Although we know a little about what Joseph does, we do not know much at all about *who* this man really is on the inside. What Joseph is thinking, hoping, or fearing about his wife's extraordinary pregnancy and his own unique calling to serve as the foster father of Israel's Messiah remains, for the most part, a great mystery.

We also return to the story of Zechariah and Elizabeth as they experience the birth of their long-awaited son, John the Baptist.

Nine months after Zechariah doubted the angel's message to him in the temple, he gets a second chance to believe.

Sunday | *Humble Royalty*

> In the sixth month the angel Gabriel was sent from God
> to a city of Galilee named Nazareth, to a virgin betrothed
> to a man whose name was Joseph, of the house of David.
>
> —Luke 1:26–27

We have already noted that Matthew's genealogy presents Joseph, the husband of Mary, as coming from the house of David. Here we see that Luke also presents the fact that Joseph is part of this most famous family in Israel.

One might expect being a part of the Davidic dynasty to be a great privilege and honor in ancient Jewish culture. After all, it was David who was promised by God an everlasting kingdom (see 2 Samuel 7), and it was David's descendants who ruled God's people for hundreds of years from the throne in Jerusalem (see 1 and 2 Kings). Yet David's great dynasty seemed to come to a tragic halt in 586 B.C., when the foreign armies of Babylon invaded Jerusalem, destroyed the temple, and carried the Jews away into exile. For most of the six centuries that followed—up to the days of Mary, Joseph, and Jesus—one foreign nation after another ruled over the Jews in Palestine.

In the time of Mary and Joseph, the Jews are suffering under Roman occupation. In such oppressive conditions, being a member of David's family no longer holds the privileges, authority, and honor that it held in the glory days of the kings who reigned in Jerusalem.

This Joseph "of the house of David" is a humble carpenter, leading a quiet, ordinary life in the small town of Nazareth.

Still God remembers the words he spoke to David at the beginning of his kingship in Jerusalem:

> I will make for you a *great* name.... I will raise up your offspring after you, who shall come forth from your body, and I will establish his kingdom. He shall build a house for my name, and I will establish *the throne of his kingdom for ever. I will be his father, and he shall be my son....* And your house and *your kingdom shall be made sure for ever* before me; *your throne shall be established for ever.* (2 Samuel 7:9, 12–14, 16, emphasis added)

It is from this house of David, however humble it has become in Joseph's day, that the Messiah will come to Israel.

For Reflection

How might the example of the Lord's fidelity to the house of David strengthen my trust in God's care for my life?

> *Lord, thank you for your faithfulness to your promises throughout the generations. I know that you will always be faithful to me. Help me always be faithful to you.*

MONDAY | *Joseph—Silent Knight, Holy Knight*

When his mother Mary had been betrothed to Joseph, before they came together she was found to be with child of the Holy Spirit; and her husband Joseph, being a just man and unwilling to put her to shame, resolved to send her away quietly. But as he considered this, behold, an angel of the Lord appeared to him in a dream, saying, "Joseph, son of David, do not fear to take Mary your wife, for that which is conceived in her is of the Holy Spirit."

—Matthew 1:18–20

In this scene we catch a glimpse into the soul of this mysterious man. What is Joseph planning to do? What does it mean to "send her away quietly"? And why does he want to do it?

One interpretation of this passage holds that Joseph learns of Mary's pregnancy and assumes that she has committed adultery, since he knows the child is not his. Since Joseph is "a just man," he in the end decides to divorce her secretly in order to spare Mary the severe punishment of the law. This was the view of Church Fathers such as Sts. John Chrysostom, Ambrose, and Augustine.

A second interpretation holds that Joseph already has knowledge that Mary has conceived by the Holy Spirit. Sts. Ephraim, Basil, Bernard, and Thomas Aquinas were of this mind-set. Realizing that God is working in Mary's life in a profound way, Joseph feels inadequate to serve as Mary's husband. He desires to release her from the obligation of marriage because of his reverence for the extraordinary work God is doing in her life.

A third interpretation views Joseph as simply not knowing what to think about Mary's pregnancy. He knows Mary is with child, and he knows the baby is not his. At the same time he is certain that Mary has remained faithful to him. Joseph remains in this dilemma until the angel comes to explain where the baby came from: the Holy Spirit.

Whatever interior drama Joseph may have been experiencing before the angel appeared to him, his response to the angel's message was immediate, strong, and decisive. "When Joseph woke from sleep, he did as the angel of the Lord commanded him" (Matthew 1:24). He did not fear any longer to take Mary as his wife.

FOR REFLECTION

How do I deal with troubling dilemmas in my life? Do I wait to hear from the Lord before taking action?

St. Joseph, pray for me, that I may learn from your example of wholehearted dedication to God and his plan, even if initially I do not fully understand its purpose.

TUESDAY | *Old Joseph, New Joseph*

> Jacob [was] the father of Joseph the husband of Mary, of whom Jesus was born, who is called Christ.
>
> —Matthew 1:16

In the opening chapters of the first Gospel, Joseph seems to replay the life of another famous Joseph in the Bible, Joseph the patriarch from the book of Genesis. There are numerous parallels between these two great men. Here are a few:

First, they not only are both called Joseph, but even their fathers share a common name, Jacob (see Genesis 37:2–3). Second, both are persecuted. Joseph's brothers sell him into slavery, and King Herod tries to kill Joseph's foster son, Jesus. Third, both end up in Egypt as a result of their persecution. Joseph of old becomes a slave in Egypt, while the New Testament Joseph travels there in order to flee from Herod's terror.

Fourth, both Josephs are famous for their dreams. Joseph the patriarch is well-known for his dreams and for interpreting other people's dreams. As for the Joseph in Matthew's Gospel, it seems that every scene with him involves an angel of the Lord appearing to him in a dream and telling him to do something or go somewhere. Poor Joseph does not seem to get much sleep!

Fifth, both Josephs were known for their purity. The most famous virtue of Joseph the patriarch was his chastity, stemming from his steadfast purity while facing the temptation of Potiphar's wife.

According to Catholic tradition, Mary and Joseph remained celibate throughout the entirety of their marriage. Fittingly, Joseph has often been called Mary's "most chaste spouse."

Sixth, both Josephs are known for their role as the protector and rescuer of their families. Joseph of old ends up saving his family from starvation, while Joseph of the New Testament protects his family from the murderous plot of Herod. The latter Joseph is considered the patron saint of the Catholic Church, as he continues through his intercession to protect the holy family of God today. In the words of Pope Leo XIII:

> Joseph was in his day the lawful and natural guardian, head, and defender of the Holy Family.... It is thus fitting and most worthy of Joseph's dignity that, in the same way that he once kept unceasing holy watch over the family of Nazareth, so now does he protect and defend with his heavenly patronage the Church of Christ.

FOR REFLECTION

This Advent, how can I more fully entrust myself to the care of St. Joseph?

St. Joseph, I pray that through your intercession you may protect my family, my parish, and the Catholic Church.

WEDNESDAY | *Zechariah's Second Chance*

Now the time came for Elizabeth to be delivered, and she gave birth to a son. And her neighbors and kinsfolk heard that the Lord had shown great mercy to her, and they rejoiced with her. And on the eighth day they came to circumcise the child; and they would have named him Zechariah after his father, but his mother said, "Not so, he shall be called John." ...And they made signs to his father, inquiring what he would have him called. And he asked for a writing tablet, and wrote, "His name is John."...And immediately his mouth was opened and his tongue loosed, and he spoke, blessing God.

—Luke 1:57–60, 62–64

Let's return to the story of Zechariah, the husband of Elizabeth and the father of John the Baptist. The birth of his son is a crucial moment for Zechariah; it is the first time we see him cooperating with the Lord's plan as revealed by Gabriel. In the temple Zechariah responded to the angel's message with doubt. Now, after nine quiet months to consider the angel's words and witness their fulfillment, Zechariah has come to greater faith. He obeys the angel's command and names the child John. As soon as he does this, his punishment comes to an end. His mouth is "immediately" opened, and he can speak again.

Those present sense God's hand in these events. In awe, they recognize that they are caught up in something much larger than the circumcision and naming of this child. God must have some special purpose for the newborn. Fear of the Lord comes upon them, and they wonder, "What then will this child be?" (Luke 1:66).

FOR REFLECTION

What is one area of my life right now where I wish I had a second chance—in the way I treated someone or in a choice I made or in a failure to do something good? What can I do to get this area of my life back on the right path again?

Lord, thank you for the second chances you give your people. You are always ready to strengthen, heal, and guide us by your Holy Spirit. Help us hear your directives and respond ever more faithfully.

THURSDAY | *Benedictus*

And his father Zechariah was filled with the Holy Spirit,
and prophesied, saying,
"Blessed be the Lord God of Israel,
for he has visited and redeemed his people."

—Luke 1:67–68

Zechariah uses his newfound speech to thank God in a hymn-like prayer that has come to be known as the Benedictus (the translation of the first word in Latin of his praise, "Blessed"). This is the second canticle in Luke's Gospel and, like Mary's song in Luke 1:46–55, the Benedictus serves as a pause in the narrative, giving the reader a chance to reflect on the saving events that are taking place.

The language Zechariah uses in this hymn of praise would have stirred up much hope in the hearts of his neighbors and relatives listening that day. If we were there, we would hear in Zechariah's song an announcement that the history of the world has reached a decisive turning point and that God is about to act in our lives in a most dramatic fashion.

The first thing that might grab people's attention is Zechariah's proclamation that God has "visited" his people. This language is not about God's stopping by to say hello. Rather, the depiction of God "visiting" his people served as a powerful image in the Old Testament to describe how the Lord mercifully looked upon his people's sufferings and freed them from their afflictions (see Genesis 21:1; Exodus 4:31; Ruth 1:6; Psalm 80:14; 106:4).

For example, when God "visited" the Israelites during their slavery in Egypt, he looked upon their hardships and then sent Moses to deliver them from their foes (see Exodus 4:31). Now in the Benedictus, Zechariah is announcing similar astonishing news. God has "visited" his people again. In other words, the same saving hand that rescued Israel from the Egyptians is, in some sense, about to save the nation from its current hardships under Roman rule.

A second amazing point from Zechariah's canticle is his saying that God has "redeemed" his people. The term *redeem* originally was used to describe the Jewish custom of buying back something that once was one's own but had fallen into the hands of another. The word, in fact, means, "to buy back."

The Old Testament came to use redemption imagery spiritually, to depict God's activity of freeing his people from their enemies. In fact, the redemption story *par excellence* was the Exodus, when the Lord "bought back" the Israelites from slavery, releasing them from their oppression in Egypt.

What is most significant about the word *redemption* is that prophets such as Isaiah spoke of the Lord's performing another great act of redemption for his people in the future. The prophets foretold that one day God would *redeem* the Jews from their current enemies as he freed their ancestors from Pharaoh in the first Exodus (see, for example, Isaiah 43:1; 44:22–23; 52:9). After hundreds of years of foreign domination, Jews in the time of Zechariah would be longing for this new exodus to arrive. They would be yearning for God to fulfill the prophecies and "buy them back" from their oppression. Therefore, when Zechariah speaks of God's *redeeming* his people, he is proclaiming that the long-awaited new exodus is finally here!

FOR REFLECTION

How might God want to "visit" me with his saving hand as he did the ancient Israelites? From what might he want to redeem me?

Lord of the universe, thank you for never giving up your pursuit of human hearts. Thank you for your faithfulness. Help me to be open to your visits.

Friday | *A Horn of Salvation*

The Lord God of Israel

…

has raised up a horn of salvation for us
in the house of his servant David.

—Luke 1:68, 69

Here Zechariah's song reaches a climactic point. These words
would have signaled that God is now sending the much-anticipated
Messiah to restore the kingdom to Israel.

In the ancient Near East the horn was a symbol of strength.
However, when Zechariah speaks of a horn rising *in the house of his
servant David*, he has a very specific power in mind—the strength of
a new King coming from the Davidic dynasty. In fact, Zechariah's
words echo the royal hymn of Psalm 132, which celebrated God's
covenant with King David and his descendants: "I will make a horn
to sprout for David; / I have prepared a lamp for my anointed"
(Psalm 132:17).

What kind of salvation will this Messiah bring? The emphasis
in the first half of Zechariah's song appears to be on a military or
political liberation. Zechariah portrays this salvation in terms of
the Israelites being "saved from our enemies, / and from the hand
of all who hate us" (Luke 1:71). Similarly, he says Israel will be
"delivered from the hand of our enemies" (1:74). For many Jews in
Zechariah's day, "our enemies" and "all who hate us" easily would

be identified as Rome, Herod, and all those in league with these first-century oppressors of the Jewish people.

However, we will see clearly in the second half of Zechariah's song, the Benedictus, that the new Davidic King will not be leading a political revolution or military takeover. Instead he comes to offer a much more profound type of liberation, a spiritual one that will enable us to truly "serve him without fear, / in holiness and righteousness before him all the days of our life" (Luke 1:74–75).

FOR REFLECTION

What bonds keep me from a life of joy and holiness in the power of the Holy Spirit?

Lord Jesus, you set us free from all the snares of the world, the flesh, and the devil. Help me live in that freedom by rejecting these snares and following you faithfully.

Saturday | *True Freedom*

> And you, child, will be called the prophet of the Most
> High; for you will go before the Lord to prepare his ways,
> to give knowledge of salvation to his people
> in the forgiveness of their sins.
>
> —Luke 1:76–77

These verses represent Zechariah's first words to his eight-day-old son. Here he finally proclaims in front of all his neighbors and family members what the angel Gabriel told him privately in the inner courts of the temple nine months ago: His son will be Israel's last and greatest prophet—the one who will prepare the way for the Lord.

Zechariah goes on to say that John the Baptist's mission as the Messiah's forerunner is to give people "knowledge of salvation." And he makes clear where this salvation will be found: not in political action or military maneuvering but "in the forgiveness of their sins." This is the first time in Luke's Gospel that God's plan of salvation for Israel is explicitly linked with the forgiveness of sins.

Zechariah's song reminds all of us that we should see the sufferings of the world not only on a political or social level but primarily on a spiritual one. The root problem for all social injustices lies in the hearts of men and women, and it is the spiritual illness there that God wants to treat. This is the illness that keeps the human family from true solidarity and from full union with God.

The next time Zechariah's son appears in Luke's Gospel, he will be grown up and already out in the wilderness preparing the way of the Lord. He will be "preaching a baptism of repentance for the forgiveness of sins" (Luke 3:3), just as his father foretells in the Benedictus.

FOR REFLECTION

What are the roots of today's social ills? What should change in my heart so that I can be more of an instrument of Christ's love in our broken world?

Lord, I repent of all my sin and come to you for forgiveness. Purify my heart, that I might "serve you without fear."

WEEK THREE

In Mary's Footsteps: Her Call and Her Journey of Faith

This week, the focus is on Mary, the Mother of Jesus. We will walk with her from the Annunciation to her visit to Elizabeth. But first, what was Mary's life like originally—*before* she learned that she was to become the Mother of Israel's Messiah?

While Luke's Gospel does not offer a lot of information, it does tell us that she lived in the town of Nazareth. This was a small village in the region of Galilee. It was not a famous place, and Jesus's coming from such an obscure village would cause him trouble later in his public ministry. Some would question how he really could be sent from God, since no prophet ever came out of this region (see John 7:52), while others would wonder whether anything good at all could come out of this little town (see John 1:46).

Second, Luke describes Mary as *betrothed* to a man by the name of Joseph. At her betrothal Mary would have consented before public witnesses to marry Joseph, and this would have established the couple as husband and wife. As a betrothed wife, however, Mary would have continued to live with her own family, apart from her husband, for up to a year. Only after this would the second stage of marriage take place—the consummation of the marriage and the wife's moving into the husband's home.

Perhaps even more noteworthy, however, is the fact that women in first-century Palestine generally were betrothed in their early teen years. This tells us that Mary probably was a very young woman when God called her to serve as the Mother of the Messiah.

But the most striking point we know about Mary's life prior to the Annunciation is that she was to marry a man from "the house of David" (1:27). It is from this house that God has promised to send the Messiah.

SUNDAY | *Troubling Words*

> The angel Gabriel...came to her and said, "Hail, full of
> grace, the Lord is with you!" But she was greatly troubled
> at the saying, and considered in her mind what sort of
> greeting this might be.
>
> —Luke 1:26, 28–29

Mary's world was about to radically change.

Imagine being home alone, walking into a room, and finding an angel suddenly standing before you! Anyone would be "greatly troubled" by the appearance of a heavenly visitor such as this. However, Luke's Gospel tells us that Mary is not startled simply by the angel itself but by the angel's *greeting*. Why might Mary be so anxious about the angel's words? Let's consider two points.

First the angel says, "Hail, full of grace." No one else in the Bible has ever been honored by an angel with such an exalted title. The Greek word *kecharitomene*, which here is translated "full of grace," indicates that Mary already possesses God's saving grace. The Lord has prepared her as a pure and holy temple in which the divine Christ child will dwell for nine months.

Second, the angel says, "The Lord is with you!" Although many Catholics today are accustomed to hearing "The Lord be with you" repeated throughout the Mass, we might not be as familiar with the powerful significance these words originally had in ancient Judaism. In fact, these words often accompanied an invitation from God to play a crucial role in his plan of salvation. Such a divine calling generally entailed great sacrifices and challenged people to step out of their comfort zones and put their trust in God as never before.

At the same time, these words offered assurance that they would not face these challenges alone. They would not have to rely solely on their own abilities and talents, because God's presence and protection would be with them throughout their mission. Some of Israel's greatest leaders—men like Isaac, Jacob, Joshua, Gideon, and David—were told that God would be with them when they were commissioned to serve his people.

With these words Mary probably realizes that a lot is being asked of her. At the same time, the greeting tells her that she will not have to face these difficulties alone. God gives her the one thing she needs most: the assurance that he will be with her.

FOR REFLECTION

In light of the biblical background for the words "The Lord be with you," what does this prayer of the priest at Mass tell me about *my* mission as a Christian?

Lord, help me remember that you are with me in my Christian vocation. Make me aware of your Spirit's guidance, and give me courage to step out of my comfort zone and trust in you more.

MONDAY | *Favor with God*

> And the angel said to her, "Do not be afraid, Mary, for you
> have found favor with God."
>
> —Luke 1:30

Through the words of the angel, we learn more of Mary's mission. Like the phrase "The Lord is with you," the notion of finding "favor with God" also would bring to mind a whole roster of Old Testament covenant mediators who were set apart for a special mission in God's plan of salvation. It describes someone to whom God has entrusted much.

Noah was the first person in the Bible described as finding favor with God (see Genesis 6:8). God saved him and his family from the flood and gave him a covenant to be the head of a renewed human family. The next person to find favor with God was Abraham (see Genesis 18:2–3). God made a covenant with him, calling on his family to be the instrument through which he would bring blessing to all the nations of the world. Similarly, Moses, the covenant mediator who led Israel out of slavery in Egypt, found favor with God (see Exodus 33:12–17), as did David, for whom God established a kingdom (see 2 Samuel 15:25).

Like these great covenant mediators of the Old Testament, Mary has found favor with God. Walking in the footsteps of Noah, Abraham, Moses, and David, Mary now is called to serve as an important cooperator in the divine plan to bring salvation to all the nations.

In fact, the angel tells Mary, "You will conceive in your womb and bear a son.... He will be great, and will be called the Son of the Most High" (Luke 1:31, 32).

Mary will bear a Son who will bring Israel's history to its climax. She will be the Mother of Israel's long awaited Messiah-King.

For Reflection

How well am I fulfilling the responsibilities God has entrusted to me—in my family, my work, my parish, or my community? What can I do to live these out more faithfully "in God's favor"?

Dear Lord, this Advent season, help me to be a better steward of what you've entrusted to me. Show me ways to be more faithful wherever you have placed me.

TUESDAY | *What Child Is This?*

> Mary said to the angel, "How can this be, since I have no
> husband?" And the angel said to her,
> "The Holy Spirit will come upon you,
> and the power of the Most High will overshadow you;
> therefore the child to be born will be called holy,
> the Son of God."
>
> —Luke 1:34–35

Gabriel underscores the extraordinary type of motherhood to
which Mary is being called, and we are given the first clear indica-
tion of the virginal conception of the Messiah.

Furthermore, we see that Jesus's filial relationship with God far
surpasses that of any king in David's dynasty. Jesus will be called Son
of God not simply because of his role as Davidic heir (see 2 Samuel
7:14; Psalm 2:7; Psalm 89:26–27) and Messiah but because of his
unique divine origin. As the *Catechism* explains:

> In fact, the One whom [Mary] conceived as man by the
> Holy Spirit, who truly became her Son according to the
> flesh, was none other than the Father's eternal Son, the
> second person of the Holy Trinity. Hence the Church
> confesses that Mary is truly "Mother of God" (*Theotokos*).
>
> —*CCC*, 495

The Church Fathers also saw the virginal conception as a sign that the divine Son of God really became human, taking the flesh of his Mother, Mary. God did not just *appear* as a man, but he truly became one of us in Jesus, experiencing birth, life, suffering, and even death.

FOR REFLECTION

Do I recognize Jesus as both the divine Son of God and the human Son of Man—the God who truly became one of us?

Come, Lord Jesus. Reign in power and might over your people. Capture our hearts so that we can be faithful members of your kingdom.

WEDNESDAY | *Mary's* Fiat

And Mary said, "Behold, I am the handmaid of the Lord; let it be to me according to your word." And the angel departed from her.

—Luke 1:38

Think of all that Mary just learned: She will soon be expecting a baby, this child is the long-awaited Messiah who will restore Israel's kingdom and bring the history of the world to its climactic moment, she will conceive not through natural means but by the Holy Spirit, and the child will be the divine Son of God. That's a lot to swallow in one short conversation with an angel!

What is interesting about Mary's response is that the Greek word in this verse for "let it be to me" expresses not a passive acceptance but a joyful wishing or desiring on Mary's part. Upon hearing of her extraordinary maternal mission, she positively desires it and fully embraces God's call.

This is why many scholars—Catholic and Protestant alike—recognize Mary as the first Christian disciple and a model follower of Jesus. In Luke's Gospel, Jesus says that those who hear the word of God and keep it are blessed and are included in his family of disciples (see Luke 8:21). Mary fits this description better than anyone else in Luke's Gospel. From the very beginning, she accepts God's word from the angel Gabriel and calls herself the servant of the Lord. In subsequent scenes we will see that Mary responds promptly to her relative Elizabeth's needs as soon as she learns from Gabriel that Elizabeth is pregnant in her old age.

Furthermore, she is counted among the "blessed" disciples in Luke's Gospel. Not only will Elizabeth call Mary blessed for believing God's word (1:45), but Mary herself will say that *all generations* will call her blessed (1:48). Similarly, like a good disciple who hears God's word and keeps it, Mary will "keep in her heart" the angel's joyous message at Jesus's birth (2:19) and Christ's words to her when she finds him in the temple (2:51).

Finally, in the Acts of the Apostles, Luke shows Mary persevering in faithfulness, devoting herself to prayer and to the life of the early Christian community in the days following her Son's Resurrection and Ascension into heaven (see Acts 1:14). Throughout her life, therefore, Mary's acceptance of God's word is exemplary. This is one reason why we consider Mary to be not only the first Christian disciple but the most perfect disciple of all time. Her obedience anticipates the response many will make to Christ's call to follow him in his public ministry and throughout the Christian era.

Her faith also serves as a model for how we as Christians should follow Christ today. Like Mary, we should respond to God's word promptly, joyfully, and with a servant's heart—not simply with a passive acceptance but with an active embrace and hunger to do God's will.

FOR REFLECTION

Is there an area in my life where I can imitate Mary and more joyfully embrace God's will?

> *Lord, help me to be more like Mary and to lovingly seek to live my life for your purposes, not just my own.*

THURSDAY | *Blessed Among Women*

In those days Mary arose and went with haste into the hill country, to a city of Judah, and she entered the house of Zechariah and greeted Elizabeth. And when Elizabeth heard the greeting of Mary, the child leaped in her womb; and Elizabeth was filled with the Holy Spirit and she exclaimed with a loud cry, "Blessed are you among women, and blessed is the fruit of your womb!"

—Luke 1:39–42

Mary is a wonderful example of a blessed disciple in action. Mary's own pregnancy does not keep her from going to help Elizabeth in her time of need.

Filled with the Holy Spirit, Elizabeth has prophetic insight into the uniqueness of Mary's motherhood. Not only does she realize that Mary is pregnant, but she understands that Mary has become the Mother of Israel's Messiah. In awe over the mystery taking place in Mary's womb, Elizabeth, in extraordinary fashion, honors her younger kinswoman and acknowledges her as "the mother of my Lord" and "blessed among women."

Let us consider what these titles would have meant in ancient Judaism. "My Lord" was a court expression given to honor the anointed king (see, for example, 2 Samuel 24:21; Psalm 110:1). Thus, when Elizabeth addresses Mary as "the mother of my Lord," she is recognizing her as the royal mother of Israel's Messiah. And this is no small honor, for as the mother of the King, Mary would be seen as the queen in her Son's kingdom. In the ancient kingdom of Judah, the queenship was given not to the king's wife but to the king's mother. And significantly, the Queen Mother served as an advocate for the people who brought their petitions to her, and she would present them to the king (1 Kings 2:13–20). This background sheds light on Mary's intercessory role in the Church. As the Queen Mother in her Son's kingdom, Mary serves as an advocate bringing our petitions to King Jesus.

Next, the description "blessed among women" would bring to mind the Old Testament heroines Jael and Judith. After Jael defeated a pagan general who was oppressing God's people, the prophetess Deborah proclaimed, "Most blessed of women be Jael" (Judges 5:24). Similarly, when Judith defeated a pagan commander who was attempting to overtake a Jewish town, Uzziah said to her: "O daughter, you are blessed by the Most High God above all women on earth" (Judith 13:18). Jael and Judith were blessed specifically because the Lord used them to rescue his people from the attacks of their enemies.

Standing in this tradition, Mary, too, will be instrumental in God's plan for saving Israel. However, Mary's role has one crucial difference from those of these warrior women of old. Mary won't be engaging in a physical battle. Rather, she will participate in God's saving plan through the Son she is carrying in her womb.

Elizabeth tells Mary that she is "blessed among women" because "blessed is the fruit of your womb." Mary is blessed because she will bear Israel's Messiah, and he will be the one to accomplish God's ultimate plan of salvation.

For Reflection

How is my relationship with Mary, our Queen Mother? What petitions could I bring to her, knowing she is a loving intercessor for us with her Son, Jesus?

> *Hail Mary, full of grace, the Lord is with thee.*
> *Blessed art thou among women, and blessed is the fruit of thy womb, Jesus.*
> *Holy Mary, Mother of God, pray for us sinners, now and at the hour of our death. Amen.*

FRIDAY | *The Ark of the Covenant*

Elizabeth…exclaimed with a loud cry, "…And why is this granted me, that the mother of my Lord should come to me?"

—Luke 1:41, 42, 43

Luke's narrative highlights Jesus's exalted status most profoundly by portraying his Mother in ways that would recall for the first-century Jew the most sacred vessel in all of Israel: the ark of the covenant.

The ark had housed three objects of great importance: a jar containing the manna that fed the Israelites in the time of Moses; the remains of the stone tablets upon which God had written the Ten Commandments; and the staff of Aaron, the first high priest of Israel (see Hebrews 9:4). Most importantly, the holy presence of God hovered over the ark in the form of a cloud.

Even before the Visitation scene, Luke's Gospel hints at parallels between Mary and the ark. In Luke 1:35 the angel Gabriel tells Mary "the power of the Most High will overshadow you." The Greek verb Luke uses for *overshadow* is the same verb used in Exodus 40:35 to describe how God's presence and glory in the form of a cloud overshadowed the sanctuary, which housed the ark of the covenant.

Luke's portrayal of Mary's journey to visit Elizabeth brings to mind a climactic moment from the life of David. David went up from Baale-judah (the hill country of Judea) to bring the ark of the covenant to Jerusalem (see 2 Samuel 6:2). On the way there David, in awe of God's power in the ark, paused and said, "How can the ark of the Lord come to me?" (6:9). The ark remained in the house of Obededom for three months, blessing Obededom and all his household (6:10–11). Then the ark was brought up to Jerusalem in a grand procession, with the people rejoicing and shouting (6:15) and with King David himself leaping and dancing before it (6:16).

Just like the ark, Mary traveled to the hill country of Judah (Luke 1:39). Mary remained in the house of Zechariah (Luke 1:40) about three months (Luke 1:56). As the people in Jerusalem welcomed the ark with shouting and rejoicing, so Elizabeth "exclaimed with a loud cry" when she greeted Mary (Luke 1:42). And John the Baptist *leapt* in Elizabeth's womb when Mary drew near (Luke 1:41).

Finally, just as David asked on the ark's arrival, "How can the ark of the Lord come to me?" so Elizabeth welcomed Mary, "And why is this granted to me, that the mother of my Lord should come to me?" (Luke 1:43).

Perhaps the most striking parallel between Mary and the ark of the covenant comes in Luke 1:42, which tells us that Elizabeth "exclaimed" when she greeted Mary. The Greek verb for *exclaim* that Luke chose for this verse (*anaphonein*) is used almost every-where else in the Bible to depict the shouting of the Levitical priests in song and praise before the ark of the covenant. Like those Levites of old, Elizabeth shouts praises (*anaphonein*) before her Lord, residing in Mary's womb. Luke thus portrays Mary like the ark of the covenant—and fittingly so.

Just as the ark carried the manna, so Mary carries in her womb the child who will be known as the true Bread of Life (see John 6:48–51). Just as the ark contained the Ten Commandments, so Mary bears the One who is the fulfillment of the Law (see Matthew 5:17). And just as the ark carried the staff of the high priest Aaron, so does Mary carry in her womb the true High Priest who will offer his life on the cross for our sins (see Hebrews 8:1–7).

FOR REFLECTION

Today's reflection shows how an attentive reading of the Bible can draw out the beautiful connections between the Old and New Testaments and the unity of God's plan. How can I make Scripture study a more regular part of my life?

Lord, thank you for your inspired Word in Scripture. Help me appreciate all the wonders of your plan of salvation as it unfolds in the Bible.

WEEK FOUR

(December 17–23)

From Nazareth to Bethlehem: The Joys and Sorrows of the Holy Family

As we enter the final week before the celebration of Christ's coming, Mary's hymn of praise, the Magnificat, invites us to reflect on all the dramatic events that have been rapidly unfolding before us at the dawn of Christianity.

We also take a look at some of the circumstances of Christ's birth. God had the power to choose the specific place and time of his Son's arrival, and he chose to have him born in conditions of extreme poverty. The *Catechism of the Catholic Church* (525) says, "In this poverty heaven's glory was made manifest."

Is this the glory we seek at Christmas?

DECEMBER 17 | *The Magnificat*

Mary said,

"My soul magnifies the Lord,

and my spirit rejoices in God my Savior."

—Luke 1:46

If we were living in first-century Judea, many of the words from Mary's song would sound very familiar to our ears. It would seem somewhat like a remake of an "oldie" from the Jewish tradition— the song of Hannah on becoming the mother of Samuel after years of barrenness.

Hannah's song begins:

My heart exults in the LORD;

my strength is exalted in the LORD. (1 Samuel 2:1)

Both songs praise the Lord as Savior and acknowledge him as holy. Both go on to announce how the mighty and rich will be cast down, while the lowly and the poor will be raised up. Those who have their fill will come away empty, while the hungry will hunger no more. These parallels demonstrate that Mary views herself as standing in the tradition of women like Hannah whom God has raised up from their afflictions.

Like Hannah, Mary has conceived a child through the miraculous intervention of God in her life. Like Hannah, Mary will dedicate her Son in the temple (see Luke 2:22–24). Like Hannah, Mary responds with a song of praise and thanksgiving for the providential child she is given.

Hannah's song culminates with the announcement of the future coming of a king (see Samuel 2:10). Mary's song, on the other hand, rejoices in the fact that God has fulfilled the promise "he spoke to our fathers" of the long-awaited Messiah-King, whom she now carries in her womb.

For Reflection

If I had a song of praise like Hannah and Mary did, for what would I thank the Lord?

Lord, I make Mary's and Hannah's songs my own. I, too, praise and thank you for the blessings you have bestowed upon my life.

DECEMBER 18 | *God Remembers*

He has regarded the low estate of his handmaiden.

For behold, henceforth all generations will call me blessed;

for he who is mighty has done great things for me,

and holy is his name.

And his mercy is on those who fear him

from generation to generation.

—Luke 1:48–50

In this first half of the Magnificat, the camera focuses on Mary. The particular word Mary uses for her "low estate" (*tapeinosin*) describes not simply a spiritual humility but a condition of great suffering. In fact, the word was commonly used in the Old Testament to depict the affliction of God's people when they were persecuted and oppressed but about to be rescued by God's saving hand (see Deuteronomy 26:7; 1 Samuel 9:16; 2 Kings 14:26). For example, recalling how God once freed Israel from its slavery in Egypt, Psalm 136 says:

It is he who remembered us in our *low estate...*

and rescued us from our foes.

(Psalm 136:23–24, emphasis added)

Considered within the social context of Roman and Herodian rule in first-century Galilee, Mary's "low estate" would bring to mind the pains experienced by many Jews who were suffering under foreign domination at that time. As one New Testament scholar has explained, "It is not that Mary has some personal and individual affliction; her affliction is simply that of God's people awaiting his saving intervention on their behalf."

This prepares the way for understanding the second half of Mary's song, where the camera lens is pulled back so that we can see God's people as a whole—the people who have Mary as their premier member. Mary announces that what God has done for her he is about to do for all those of "low degree" (*tapeinous*) in Israel (1:52). God has remembered his covenant with Abraham and has come to help his people Israel (1:54–55).

FOR REFLECTION

What areas of my life might be of "low estate"? How does God regard me in those areas?

Dear Lord, thank you for the example of your Mother, "blessed among women" yet your handmaiden of "low estate," yet "blessed among women." Help me see things as she did—through your eyes.

December 19 | *Song of the Church*

He has shown strength with his arm,

he has scattered the proud in the imagination of their
hearts,

he has put down the mighty from their thrones,

and exalted those of low degree;

he has filled the hungry with good things,

and the rich he has sent empty away.

—Luke 1:51–53

To understand more fully what Mary is saying in this part of the
Magnificat, it is important to note that in Luke's Gospel, the words
rich and *poor* are not simply economic terms. "The hungry" here
refers not only to people in material poverty but, more broadly,
to all the marginalized and downtrodden in society. Throughout
Luke's Gospel, in fact, "the poor" refers to a wide range of people,
including the blind, the lame, the deaf, and the lepers, as well as
those burdened by sociopolitical injustices such as "the oppressed,"
"the captives," "the persecuted," and "the hungry." In a similar
manner, "the rich" is not simply a synonym for the economic upper
class but a social term describing those who exploit, overlook, or
marginalize the various "poor" outcasts of society.

In light of this background, Mary is announcing a series of ironic
reversals in society. God in his mercy has remembered the suffering
and oppressed in Israel and will gather them into the kingdom

of his Son, while "the proud," "the mighty," and "the rich," who oppose God's people, are about to be cast down.

Mary's song anticipates the major components of her Son's mission. As the subsequent chapters of Luke's Gospel will show, Jesus's public ministry embodies these dramatic reversals proclaimed by the Magnificat, whether it be in his healing the sick, feeding the hungry, extending fellowship to the estranged, and forgiving sinners, or in his confronting the social, political, and religious leaders of the day. In fact, right at the heart of his teachings about the kingdom, we find Jesus proclaiming the same news of salvation announced in Mary's song. In the Beatitudes he announces blessing upon the poor, the hungry, the persecuted, and the excluded, while he announces woe to the rich—those who are comfortable, socially accepted, and having their fill (see Luke 6:20–26). Mary's Magnificat finds fulfillment in Christ's public ministry.

Mary's song also anticipates the prayer of the Church, which ceaselessly "proclaims the greatness of the Lord." What God has done for this lowly woman of Galilee he will do for all of us through her Son. He will meet us in our own lowliness and sufferings and do "great things" for us. Like a representative of all the faithful, Mary stands at the gateway of the new covenant as the first Christian disciple to receive the amazing mercy of God in Jesus.

For Reflection

In what ways have I seen God "exalt those of low degree" and "fill the hungry with good things"?

Dear God, show me how I can be used by you to help meet the pressing needs I see around me.

DECEMBER 20 | *Royal Decree*

In those days a decree went out from Caesar Augustus that all the world should be enrolled. This was the first enrollment, when Quirinius was governor of Syria. And all went to be enrolled, each to his own city.

—Luke 2:1–3

As we approach our celebration of Christmas, we move now to Bethlehem, where the stage is being set for the birth of God's Son.

Highlighting Christ's universal mission, Luke places the birth of Jesus on the worldwide stage of Caesar Augustus's call for a census throughout the empire. The purpose of such a census would be to regularize the collection of taxes. Luke draws our attention to this census, mentioning it four times in verses 1–6, thereby giving more information about the enrollment than about the actual birth of Jesus.

Why does Luke focus on the census? Being forced to submit to a Roman enrollment and to pay the required taxes would have been a difficult reminder for the Jews of their oppressed condition under Roman rule. For Luke's Gospel, the census thus serves as a symbol of Rome's control over Israel and the rest of the world. In a single decree, Augustus makes his presence felt by families throughout the empire, who are uprooted and forced to travel to their ancestral towns to participate in the emperor's census.

Augustus was famous for reuniting the Roman Empire and restoring peace. After the assassination of Julius Caesar in 44 B.C., Rome was thrown into political upheaval as different factions vied for power. Augustus eventually emerged as the sole ruler of Rome, bringing an end to the wars that plagued the empire.

In the eyes of many, Augustus saved Rome from destruction. He was thus hailed as "savior of the whole world," for he ushered in a new age—the age of the *Pax Romana* (the Roman Peace). He eventually was called "son of God" and worshiped as a deity. His date of birth even was celebrated in some parts of the empire as "the birthday of the god," for his coming was said to bring "good news" for the whole world.

Luke's Gospel tells a different story about the climax of the world's history. The birthday that inaugurated a new era for the world took place not in a palace in Rome but in a little dwelling in Bethlehem. And the real Savior didn't bring peace to the nations through Roman force and domination but by becoming a man, so that he might offer his life on the cross to free us from our sins.

Indeed, Luke subverts the imperial propaganda by showing how Jesus—not Caesar—is the true "Son of God" (see 1:35) and the real Lord and "Savior" of the world (2:11). Jesus is the one who brings true "peace" on earth (2:14) and whose day of birth brings "good news," marking the dawn of a new period in the history of humanity (2:10).

For Reflection

How well do I allow Jesus to reign as king over my life?

Lord, you are my true king. This Christmas, I invite you to reign in every area of my life.

DECEMBER 21 | *The City of David*

And Joseph also went up from Galilee, from the city of
Nazareth, to Judea, to the city of David, which is called
Bethlehem, because he was of the house and lineage of
David, to be enrolled with Mary, his betrothed, who was
with child. And while they were there, the time came for
her to be delivered.

—Luke 2:4–6

One of the families on the move as a result of Augustus's decree
of a census is Joseph's. Being from the house and lineage of David,
Joseph must travel to Bethlehem. He takes his pregnant wife with
him to be enrolled in "the city of David."

On one level, the story of Mary and Joseph's traveling to
Bethlehem highlights Caesar's worldwide dominance, which
reaches all the way into the life of this couple from Nazareth forced
to leave home in spite of the imminent birth of their child. On
another level, however, Luke is showing that there is someone else
who is *really* in control of the world's affairs. For Caesar's powerful
decree ironically serves God's larger plan for the Messiah-King to
be born in his proper city, Bethlehem.

Bethlehem had royal significance for the Jews. It was the city
where David was born and was anointed king (see 1 Samuel 16:1–
13). Most of all, Bethlehem had been associated with longings for
the Messiah ever since the prophet Micah foretold that a new king

would come to reunite the people of Israel and reign over all the nations. According to Micah, this new royal son, like David, would be born in Bethlehem:

> But you, O Bethlehem Ephrathah,
>> who are little to be among the clans of Judah,
> from you shall come forth for me
>> one who is to be ruler in Israel,
> whose origin is from of old,
>> from ancient days. (Micah 5:2)

Caesar, in his show of might with the worldwide census, unwittingly ends up serving the purposes of an even more powerful ruler, God himself. As a result of Caesar's decree, Mary and Joseph are brought to Bethlehem and prophecy is fulfilled as a new king is born in the city of David.

For Reflection

Do I see God as being in charge of my life? In control of what happens in the world?

Lord, help me accept the challenges of this life with a firm belief in your love for me and in your power to bring all to the good.

DECEMBER 22 | *No Room for Jesus*

There was no place for them in the inn.

—Luke 2:7

What was the actual setting in which Jesus was born?

Luke's Gospel does not clearly settle this question. The Greek word translated "inn," *katalyma*, actually has a broader meaning, denoting any place of lodging. One possibility is that *katalyma* here refers to a travelers' inn, believed to be located near Bethlehem (see Jeremiah 41:17). A primitive Palestinian inn would have housed large groups of travelers under one roof, where guests would have slept on cots alongside the animals. In this view, Mary and Joseph could not find room in the travelers' inn, so they went somewhere else to have the baby.

Another possibility is that *katalyma* refers to some type of guest room. Since Joseph is visiting his family's ancestral town, one might expect him to stay, not at an inn for travelers, but at the home of one of his relatives. In many peasant homes in ancient Palestine, people and animals slept in one enclosed space, with the family sleeping on a higher level and the animals residing below them. In this view, since there was no place to lay the baby in the presumably crowded sleeping quarters (*katalyma*), Mary put him in the manger, which would have been on the lower level of the home.

A third possibility is based on an early tradition, going back to the second century, that there was no lodging within Bethlehem, so Joseph brought Mary to a cave near the village. This is at least plausible, since caves sometimes served as housing for Palestinian peasants and their animals.

While the precise type of housing that sheltered Jesus at his birth may remain a mystery, the one thing Luke does make clear is that it was a humble place. Mary, the Immaculate Conception and Queen of Heaven and Earth, gave birth to the Messiah-King in conditions of poverty, in or near the town of Bethlehem, far from home.

FOR REFLECTION

How do I respond when I am neglected or refused a favor? How does the Lord want me to respond?

Lord, help me learn from you and Mary and Joseph to respond humbly when I am not treated well, and to see these occasions as opportunities to unite myself to your littleness, humility, and poverty in Bethlehem.

DECEMBER 23 | *Emmanuel*

"Behold, a virgin shall conceive and bear a son,
and his name shall be called Emmanuel"
(which means, God with us).

—Matthew 1:23

Matthew quotes this famous Emmanuel prophecy from the book of Isaiah (7:14) and reveals its fulfillment in Jesus. Isaiah uttered this prophecy during a crisis in the kingdom of Judah in the eighth century B.C. Foreign armies threatened to invade Jerusalem and destroy the kingdom. The Jewish king, Ahaz, feared that the Davidic dynasty might be coming to an end and that he would be the last of its kings (see Isaiah 7:1–12). Isaiah's prophecy, however, offered hope for the kingdom in these dark times.

The prophecy is sometimes seen as having an initial fulfillment in the son of Ahaz, King Hezekiah, who "did what was right in the eyes of the Lord" (2 Kings 18:3) and witnessed the dynasty's survival through crisis. But Hezekiah's reforms did not last, and the kingdom of Judah eventually was destroyed by another invading force, Babylon. Jews then would have seen how this prophecy was associated with God's larger plan to send a new anointed son of David to establish an everlasting dynasty that would reign over all the nations (see Isaiah 9; 11; 2 Samuel 7:8–17).

But Matthew clearly views Jesus, the new royal son of David, born of the Virgin Mary, as the ultimate fulfillment of this prophecy from Isaiah. Jesus will be the one to restore the kingdom and bring Israel's history to its climax. God will be with him as he promised to be with the house of David. Hence he shall be called Emmanuel, "God with us."

We, too, can delight in this mystery of Emmanuel as God continues to be present to us today. He is present in the Scriptures, in prayer, in the sacraments, and especially in the Eucharist (see *CCC*, 1373). In fact, we can see Christ's desire to be with us until the end of time in his very last words to the apostles in Matthew's Gospel:

> Go therefore and make disciples of all nations, baptizing them in the name of the Father and of the Son and of the Holy Spirit, teaching them to observe all that I have commanded you; and behold, I am with you always, to the close of the age. (Matthew 28:19–20)

FOR REFLECTION

In these last days before Christmas, how can I draw near to the God who has sought to be close to us in prayer, the Scriptures, and the sacraments?

I thank you that you seek us out and desire to be close to us in your Word and in your sacraments

CHRISTMAS

Witnesses to the Mystery:
The Shepherds, the Magi, and Simeon

The following proclamation is often made at the opening of the Catholic Church's liturgy of the Midnight Mass for Christmas Eve, to remind us that Christ's birth in Bethlehem really is the turning point of the history of the world:

> Today, the twenty-fifth day of December,
> unknown ages from the time
> when God created the heavens and the earth
> and then formed man and woman in his own image.
> Several thousand years after the flood,
> when God made the rainbow shine forth
> as a sign of the covenant.
> Twenty-one centuries from the time of Abraham and Sarah;
> thirteen centuries after Moses led the people of Israel out of Egypt.
> Eleven hundred years from the time of Ruth and the Judges;
> one thousand years from the anointing of David as king;

in the sixty-fifth week according to the prophecy of Daniel.

In the one hundred and ninety-fourth Olympiad;

the seven hundred and fifty-second year from the foundation of the city of Rome.

The forty-second year of the reign of Octavian Augustus;

the whole world being at peace,

Jesus Christ, eternal God and Son of the eternal Father,

desiring to sanctify the world by his most merciful coming,

being conceived by the Holy Spirit,

and nine months having passed since his conception,

was born in Bethlehem of Judea of the Virgin Mary.

Today is the nativity of our Lord Jesus Christ,

according to the flesh.

As we enter the Christmas season, we will walk with the Holy
Family through the biblical accounts of Christ's birth and infancy.
We journey with them from Bethlehem on that first Christmas
night to the temple for the presentation, to Egypt as they escape the
wrath of Herod, and then back to their home in Nazareth.

DECEMBER 24, CHRISTMAS EVE | *A Night to Remember*

> And in that region there were shepherds out in the field,
> keeping watch over their flock by night. And an angel
> of the Lord appeared to them, and the glory of the Lord
> shone around them, and they were filled with fear. And the
> angel said to them, "Be not afraid; for behold, I bring you
> good news of a great joy which will come to all the people;
> for to you is born this day in the city of David a Savior,
> who is Christ the Lord."
>
> —Luke 2:8–11

Can you imagine what these shepherds experienced during the
night watch in the countryside? An angel of the Lord appears in
the darkness, and they find themselves encircled by "the glory of
the Lord."

In the Old Testament God's "glory" was the visible manifestation
of his divine presence. It often appeared in the form of a cloud,
and it was associated with God's presence covering the ark of the
covenant and filling the Holy of Holies of the temple (see Exodus
40:34; 1 Kings 8:11; Ezekiel 10:4, 18). No wonder the shepherds
respond in fear! The splendid display illuminates the night, reminiscent of Zechariah's song, which foretold that the Messiah would
"give light to those who sit in darkness" (Luke 1:79).

The birth of the Messiah escapes the notice of the powerful and
privileged in Israel, while lowly shepherds in their ordinary labor

have front-row seats to the glory of God. Even more striking is the fact that these people don't have any relationship to Mary and Joseph; they are complete strangers! This open, public proclamation of Christ's birth underscores the child's universal mission. The baby Jesus will bring blessing not just to his parents; this child will be "a great joy" for "*all* the people."

FOR REFLECTION

Where might I see God's glory—his presence—this Christmas?

Lord Jesus, thank you for bringing your presence to our cold, dark world. Please let your presence shine through me this night.

December 25, Christmas Day | *The Birth of the Messiah*

> And she gave birth to her first-born son and wrapped him
> in swaddling cloths, and laid him in a manger.
>
> —Luke 2:7

Today the true King of the World is born quietly in Bethlehem and placed in a manger, escaping the notice of most of the people he has come to save. From the creation of man and woman at the beginning of time all the way up to the reign of the Roman Empire in the first century, the story of the human family reaches its climax in the coming of this child. The Gospel accounts proclaim that God's plan for all of humanity was coming to fruition.

Interestingly, some early Christians saw in Christ's lowly beginnings a foreshadowing of his humiliating death. Just as Jesus at the start of his life was wrapped in bands of cloth and laid in a manger (see Luke 2:7), so at the end of his life he would be wrapped in a linen cloth and laid in a tomb after being crucified on Calvary (see Luke 23:53). In fact, to express this connection, some Christian iconography later depicted Christ's birthplace as looking like a sepulcher.

The name of the city of his birth, Bethlehem, presents another foreshadowing of Christ's saving work. The word means "house of bread." In this place "the bread of life…comes down from heaven, that a man may eat of it and not die" (John 6:48, 50). Just as the Son of God manifested himself to the world in Bethlehem, he presents himself to us today in the Bread of Life, the Eucharist.

FOR REFLECTION

When I receive the Eucharist today, am I aware that this is truly Jesus—Body, Blood, soul, and divinity?

Lord, your presence brought joy at Bethlehem. May I always rejoice in the gift of your Real Presence in the Eucharist every time I receive you in Holy Communion.

DECEMBER 26 | *The True Shepherd*

> When the angels went away from them into heaven, the shepherds said to one another, "Let us go over to Bethlehem and see this thing that has happened, which the Lord has made known to us." And they went with haste, and found Mary and Joseph, and the baby lying in a manger. And when they saw it they made known the saying which had been told them concerning this child; and all who heard it wondered at what the shepherds told them.
>
> —Luke 2:15–18

The shepherds have been completely transformed by this experience. As Mary responded to Gabriel's message, so they respond to the angel's message "with haste" (see 1:39; 2:16). They cannot help but praise God and then go tell others of their encounter with the baby in the manger. Thus, the shepherds become the first evangelists in Luke's Gospel.

This is not the first time God has shown extraordinary favor to shepherds. In the Old Testament, people like Jacob, Joseph, Moses, and Amos were shepherds whom God called to a special role of service for his people.

The most famous shepherd of all, however, was King David. As a boy, David tended sheep (see 1 Samuel 16:11). After the Lord raised him up to be king over Israel, David was told that he would "shepherd" God's people, the twelve tribes of Israel (see 2 Samuel 5:2).

This is why shepherd imagery became associated with the Davidic dynasty and the hopes for a Messiah-King.

The prophet Ezekiel describes how in the new covenant the people will be reunited around a new son of David, like sheep gathering around their shepherd: "And I will set up over them *one shepherd*, my servant *David*, and he shall feed them; he shall feed them and be their shepherd" (Ezekiel 34:23, emphasis added).

With this background in mind, shepherds coming to Bethlehem, the city of David, to meet the newborn Christ heighten the royal Davidic character of Jesus's birth. Now this group of Bethlehem shepherds gathers around the one true Shepherd, the new David, who will lead the flock of Israel back to the Lord.

FOR REFLECTION

How might my encounter with Jesus today transform me like the shepherds who were transformed on that first Christmas night?

Lord, you are my shepherd—the Good Shepherd. I am happy to be part of your flock, transformed by your love and care.

Sunday Within the Octave of Christmas, the Feast of the Holy Family | *In His Father's House*

> After three days they found him in the temple, sitting among
> the teachers, listening to them and asking them questions;
> and all who heard him were amazed at his understanding
> and his answers.... His mother said to him, "Son, why have
> you treated us so? Behold, your father and I have been
> looking for you anxiously." And he said to them, "...Did
> you not know that I must be in my Father's house?" ...And
> his mother kept all these things in her heart.
>
> —Luke 2:46–47, 48–49, 51

The finding of Jesus in the temple is the only account we have
about Christ's "hidden years"—the years between his infancy and
the beginning of his public ministry as a thirty-year-old adult. Why
was this the only story deemed weighty enough to be included in
the Gospel?

Within the wider context of Luke's narrative, this scene serves as
a crucial bridge connecting Christ's infancy to his public ministry
as an adult, "pre-enacting" what will take place at the end of Jesus's
life. As a twelve-year-old, Jesus made a pilgrimage to Jerusalem for
the feast of Passover. But when the feast was over, Jesus stayed behind
in Jerusalem, unbeknownst to Mary and Joseph, who assumed he
was with their extended family. After three days they found him in

the temple, sitting with the elders, who were very impressed by his understanding.

Similarly, at the culmination of his public ministry, Jesus will make one last pilgrimage to Jerusalem for the feast of Passover. Once again he will enter the temple and amaze the people with his teaching. And Mary will lose her Son again, but this time in an even more profound way as he is crucified on Calvary. However, just as in his youth, Jesus will be found on the third day when he rises from the dead.

FOR REFLECTION

Are there times when I feel Jesus is missing—times when I can't find him in the usual places (such as prayer, fellowship, or church)? What can I do during times like these to "find Jesus" again?

Lord, when you seem distant, when I don't understand what you are doing in my life, help me to ponder these things in my heart, like Mary, trusting that you are doing the Father's work in the temple of my soul.

December 27, Feast of St. John, Apostle and Evangelist | *Behold the Lamb*

> And at the end of eight days, when he was circumcised, he was called Jesus, the name given by the angel before he was conceived in the womb.
>
> And when the time came for their purification according to the law of Moses, they brought him up to Jerusalem to present him to the Lord (as it is written in the law of the Lord, "Every male that opens the womb shall be called holy to the Lord") and to offer a sacrifice according to what is said in the law of the Lord, "a pair of turtledoves, or two young pigeons."
>
> —Luke 2:21–24

Forty days after his birth in Bethlehem, Mary and Joseph bring the Son of God to the Jerusalem temple. Keep in mind that this is *his* temple—the house of the living God. Still, Jesus's entry into this most sacred building escapes the notice of most of the other pilgrims that day. He comes not in royal splendor but humbly as a child. And like everyone else, he comes as one under the Law.

In fact, it is the Jewish law that brings him to the house of God. After giving birth to a male child, a Jewish mother was considered ritually impure for forty days. During this period she was not allowed to enter the temple. When her forty days of purification were completed, she was to offer a lamb and a young pigeon to the priests at the sanctuary. If a woman could not afford a lamb, she could present two young pigeons or doves instead (see Leviticus 12:1–8).

The fact that Joseph and Mary offer "a pair of turtledoves or two young pigeons" (2:24) indicates that they are poor; they cannot afford a lamb for the sacrifice. Nevertheless, they have something much more valuable to present to God. As John Paul II pointed out, they bring to the temple "the true Lamb," the child Jesus, who will redeem humanity through his sacrifice on the cross.

FOR REFLECTION

Are there laws of God and of his Church that I ignore? How can I be more faithful and obedient to these laws?

Lord, as Mary and Joseph presented Jesus in the temple and offered their humble sacrifice, I offer all that I have to you, including my obedience to your law and faithfulness to the teachings of the Church.

DECEMBER 28, FEAST OF THE HOLY INNOCENTS |
Rachel Weeps

> Herod, when he saw that he had been tricked by the Wise
> Men, was in a furious rage, and he sent and killed all the
> male children in Bethlehem and in all that region who
> were two years old or under, according to the time which
> he had ascertained from the Wise Men. Then was fulfilled
> what was spoken by the prophet Jeremiah:
>> "A voice was heard in Ramah,
>> wailing and loud lamentation,
>> Rachel weeping for her children;
>> she refused to be consoled,
>> because they were no more."
>
> —Matthew 2:16–18

When Matthew mentions a line or a key phrase from an Old
Testament prophecy or story, he is alluding to a larger story and
bringing to mind a wider cultural context. The more we get in
tune with the Old Testament, the more we will hear the beautiful
harmonies of salvation history being brought to a crescendo in
Matthew's Gospel. We see this in the account of Herod's massacre
of the Holy Innocents.

King Herod was violently insecure about his position, murdering
any suspected rival and even killing three of his own sons and his
favored wife. Matthew places Herod's latest atrocity in the context

of Jeremiah 31:15, a somber verse that speaks of Rachel weeping for her children in Ramah, a city of sorrow in the Old Testament. The Babylonians established Ramah as the assembly point for leading the Jewish captives away on the road to exile (see Jeremiah 40:1)—hence the portrayal of Rachel's loud lamentations being heard there as she wept bitterly for her descendants, who were being killed or sent into slavery during the Babylonian invasion.

In light of Herod's massacre, Matthew views Bethlehem as a new city of great suffering, a new Ramah. He fittingly brings to mind the Jewish tradition of Rachel's weeping for her children, for now it is as if she is weeping once again for the holy innocents who are killed by Herod in Bethlehem.

FOR REFLECTION

What are some ways Rachel might be weeping today?

Lord, today Rachel must still weep for the millions of unborn who have been killed by abortion. Please bring an end to this evil massacre in our land.

DECEMBER 29 | *A New Moses*

> Behold, an angel of the Lord appeared to Joseph in a dream
> and said, "Rise, take the child and his mother, and flee to
> Egypt, and remain there till I tell you; for Herod is about to
> search for the child, to destroy him." And he rose and took
> the child and his mother by night, and departed to Egypt,
> and remained there until the death of Herod. This was to
> fulfil what the Lord had spoken by the prophet, "Out of
> Egypt have I called my son."
>
> —Matthew 2:13–15

Here Matthew again highlights for his readers when a prophecy is
being fulfilled by first telling a story from the life of Jesus and then
quoting from an Old Testament prophecy that Matthew reveals
has come to fulfillment in Christ. Hosea 11:1 recalls the book
of Exodus's depiction of Israel's filial-like relationship with God
and of God's rescue of his "first-born son," Israel, from slavery in
Egypt (see Exodus 4:22–23). The prophet employed this Exodus
imagery to describe the salvific work God would do for Israel in
the future—freeing the nation from its enemies once again (see
Hosea 2:14–23).

By applying this Exodus motif to the Christ child, Matthew
shows that Jesus now embodies Israel's sonship relationship with
God. As the representative of Israel, Jesus will relive the Exodus
story in his own life. Just as God's people were called out of Egypt

and brought to the Promised Land to be a light to the nations, soon Jesus will be called out of Egypt to bring Israel's worldwide mission to completion and extend God's salvation to all the earth.

Matthew 2 also presents Jesus as the new Moses. This is a fitting paradigm for Jesus, since Moses stands out in Israel's history as the savior figure *par excellence*. Like Moses, Jesus is born during a king's wicked decree to kill the Jewish male children. Like Moses, Jesus escapes Herod's murderous plot by fleeing to Egypt. Like Moses, Jesus's father is told by the angel when it is safe for Jesus to return to the land of Israel.

Just as Moses led the people through the waters of the Red Sea and into the wilderness, where they wandered for forty years, so Jesus begins his public ministry by going through the waters of the Jordan River at his baptism (see Matthew 3) and then traveling in the desert for forty days of prayer and fasting (see Matthew 4). One of the high points of Jesus's ministry is when he goes up a mountain to give a new law, the famous Sermon on the Mount (see Matthew 5–7). This is reminiscent of Moses giving the Ten Commandments to the people at Mount Sinai.

All these parallels do not simply demonstrate some vague, coincidental similarity between Moses and Jesus. For Matthew and the early Christians, the providential hand of God had written these profound connections between the two men into the fabric of the world's history. God gave Israel its first savior figure of Moses not only to rescue the people from slavery in Egypt but also to prefigure and anticipate the new messianic Savior he would send to redeem the whole world.

FOR REFLECTION

How did God prepare me to celebrate his coming at Christmas? How does he prepare me for Jesus's daily coming? How is he preparing me for his final coming?

Father, thank you for all the ways you spoke to Israel of the coming of the Savior. We see in your Word your continual love for your people and faithfulness to your promises. Prepare our hearts for our Lord's final coming in glory.

DECEMBER 30 | *Back to Nazareth*

> Joseph…took the child and his mother, and went to the
> land of Israel. But when he heard that Archelaus reigned
> over Judea in place of his father Herod, he was afraid to go
> there, and being warned in a dream he withdrew to the
> district of Galilee. And he went and dwelt in a city called
> Nazareth, that what was spoken by the prophets might be
> fulfilled, "He shall be called a Nazarene."
>
> —Matthew 2:19, 21–23

Matthew leaves us with one last fulfillment quotation in his infancy
narrative. However, there is one major problem: There is no single
text in the entire Old Testament that says the Messiah would be a
Nazarene! Is Matthew just making up a prophecy?

Let us first note that Matthew is making a play on words, drawing
on the similarities between the word *Nazareth* and the word *neser*,
which in Hebrew means "branch." This is significant because the
word *branch* was used in the Old Testament to describe the Messiah.
For example, Isaiah 11:1 says, "There shall come forth a shoot from
the stump of Jesse, / and a branch shall grow out of his roots."

As the father of King David, Jesse represents the foundation of
the Davidic dynasty. "The stump of Jesse" symbolizes the Davidic
dynasty as it appeared to come to an end after the Babylonian invasion. Isaiah offers good news: Out of the stump of Jesse a branch
shall grow. In other words, the Davidic line will continue.

Isaiah further says that one day someone anointed with the Spirit will come from this branch, and he will bring about a worldwide kingdom (see Isaiah 11:9–10). Jeremiah and Zechariah continued the tradition of describing the Messiah as a "branch" or "shoot." In this fulfillment quotation, Matthew highlights how fitting it is that Jesus—the messianic "branch" whom the prophets foretold— would be raised in the "branch-town" of Nazareth.

For Reflection

Jesus calls his followers "branches," too: "I am the vine, you are the branches. He who abides in me, and I in him, he it is that bears much fruit, for apart from me you can do nothing" (John 15:5). How can I abide in Jesus today?

Dear Jesus, you are the True Vine, and we are the branches. Help me to always draw my nourishment from you!

DECEMBER 31 | *"Comfort, Comfort My People"*

Now there was a man in Jerusalem, whose name was Simeon, and this man was righteous and devout, looking for the consolation of Israel, and the Holy Spirit was upon him. And it had been revealed to him by the Holy Spirit that he should not see death before he had seen the Lord's Christ. And inspired by the Spirit he came into the temple; and when the parents brought in the child Jesus, to do for him according to the custom of the law, he took him up in his arms and blessed God.

—Luke 2:25–28

Perhaps the most interesting detail about Simeon is that he is looking for "the consolation of Israel." This phrase brings to mind what practically every first-century Jew would be yearning for: the fulfillment of Isaiah's prophecies about God's consoling Israel and bringing an end to their sufferings under the pagan nations:

Comfort, comfort my people, says your God.
Speak tenderly to Jerusalem,
> and cry to her
that her warfare is ended,
> that her iniquity is pardoned. (Isaiah 40:1–2)

What a moment this must be for Simeon! He holds the infant Jesus in his arms and breaks out in praise of God. He announces that

Jesus is this servant of the Lord from Isaiah. Jesus will be light to the world and gather all nations back into God's covenant family.

FOR REFLECTION

Do I let the Holy Spirit guide me, as he guided Simeon? How can I be more attentive to his promptings?

Lord, thank you for the gift of your Holy Spirit, who is our Comforter and Advocate. Please help me be open to his guidance at every moment of my life.

JANUARY 1, FEAST OF MARY THE MOTHER OF GOD | *Pierced by a Sword*

> And his father and his mother marveled at what was said
> about him; and Simeon blessed them and said to Mary his
> mother,
>> "Behold, this child is set for the fall and rising of many
>> in Israel,
>> and for a sign that is spoken against
>> (and a sword will pierce through your own soul also),
>> that thoughts out of many hearts may be revealed."
>
> —Luke 2:33–35

The joy that radiates in this scene suddenly turns to sorrow. In a prophecy addressed specifically to Mary, Simeon looks at her and warns her of the difficult path that lies ahead.

First, a sword will pierce her Son. Simeon's words foreshadow the fact that Jesus's ministry will culminate in his bloody death on the cross. There, in fact, a Roman soldier will pierce his side with a sword (see John 19:34).

The second thing these words tell Mary is that the intense opposition to Jesus will affect *her* as well: "A sword will pierce through *your own soul also.*" Here we have a foreshadowing of the suffering Mary will endure in watching her Son die on the cross. John Paul II once described Simeon's words as "a second Annunciation to Mary":

[These words] tell her of the actual historical situation in which the Son is to accomplish his mission, namely, in misunderstanding and sorrow.... [Simeon] also reveals to her that she will have to live her obedience of faith in suffering, at the side of the suffering Savior, and that her motherhood will be mysterious and sorrowful.

Indeed, here at the presentation Mary receives a fuller picture of what she signed up for when she first consented to serve as the mother of the Messiah at the Annunciation. Her *fiat* in Galilee will lead her to Calvary, where she sorrowfully will witness the offering of Jesus's life on the cross.

FOR REFLECTION

Does my yes to God endure, like Mary's did, through times of sorrow, doubt, and confusion?

Lord, thank you for the gift of your Son. Help me know, love, and serve him all the days of my life. Give me the grace to persevere like Mary did during times of difficulty.

FEAST OF THE EPIPHANY | *Gold, Frankincense, and Myrrh*

Behold, the star which they had seen in the East went before them, till it came to rest over the place where the child was. When they saw the star, they rejoiced exceedingly with great joy; and going into the house they saw the child with Mary his mother, and they fell down and worshiped him. Then, opening their treasures, they offered him gifts, gold and frankincense and myrrh.

—Matthew 2:9–11

For an ancient Jew, this event from the very beginning of Christ's life signals that this child in Bethlehem already is fulfilling his role as the great Davidic king who was expected to come and extend God's kingdom to all the nations.

In this scene, Jesus fulfills Psalm 72, which describes how the son of David will have dominion over all the earth and how kings of all nations shall bow down before him and serve him, bringing him gifts of gold (see Psalm 72:10–15). He also fulfills Isaiah 60: "*Nations shall walk by your light,* / and kings to the brightness of your rising…. / They shall bring *gold and frankincense,* / and shall proclaim the praise of the LORD" (Isaiah 60:3, 6, emphasis added).

This background clues us in to the fact that as soon as Christ begins his life on earth, he already is drawing all nations together, just as the prophets foretold. The Magi represent the first of many

Gentiles scattered throughout the world who are gathered back into God's covenant family through Christ's saving mission.

Christian tradition has viewed these three gifts as symbolizing three aspects of the mystery of Jesus Christ. Gold represents a gift fit for a king, and thus points to Christ's kingship. Frankincense is a type of incense used in worshiping God, and thus points to Christ's divinity. Myrrh was a burial ointment. It thus points to Christ's humanity and, in particular, it foreshadows his death on the cross.

For Reflection

How have these meditations helped me appreciate in a deeper way the birth of Jesus in Bethlehem?

Lord, with the whole Church I welcome the dawn of the Messiah. I pray that all people will come to know you as King, God, and Savior.

Notes

1. N.T. Wright, *The New Testament and the People of God* (Minneapolis: Fortress, 1992), pp. 378–379.

2. Leo XIII, Encyclical Epistle *Quamquam pluries* (August 15, 1889) in *Leonis XIII P.M. Acta*, IX (1890), pp. 177–179. As quoted by Pope John Paul II in *Redemptoris Custos* (Boston: St. Paul, 1989), p. 33.

3. Citing the Council of Ephesus (431): DS 251.

4. Ignace De La Potterie, *Mary in the Mystery of the Covenant*, trans. Bertrand Buby, S.M. (New York: Alba, 1992), pp. 34–35.

5. John Nolland, *Word Biblical Commentary*: Luke 1–9:20 (Nashville: Thomas Nelson, 1989), p. 54.

6. Nolland, *Word Biblical Commentary*, pp. 74–77.

7. Nolland, *Word Biblical Commentary*, p. 75.

8. See Joel Green, *New Testament Theology: The Theology of the Gospel of Luke* (Cambridge, U.K.: Cambridge University Press, 1995), pp. 79–84.

9. B. Witherington, "The Birth of Jesus," in Joel Green, et al., eds., *Dictionary of Jesus and the Gospels* (Downers Grove, Ill.: InterVarsity, 1992), p. 70.

10. Green, *New Testament Theology*, p. 124.

11. John Paul II, General Audience of December 11, 1996, in John Paul II, *Theotokos: Woman, Mother, Disciple* (Boston: Pauline, 2000), p. 155.

12. See Donald A. Hagner, *Word Biblical Commentary: Matthew 1—13* (Nashville: Thomas Nelson, 1993), p. 41.

13. John Paul II, *Redemptoris Mater*, Encyclical on the Blessed Virgin Mary in the Life of the Pilgrim Church, 16, March 25, 1987, www.vatican.va.

About the Author

Edward Sri is vice president of mission and outreach and professor of theology and Scripture at the Augustine Institute in Denver and founding leader with Curtis Martin of FOCUS (Fellowship of Catholic University Students). Dr. Sri holds a doctorate from the Pontifical University of St. Thomas Aquinas in Rome. His books include *The New Rosary in Scripture: Biblical Insights for Praying the 20 Mysteries* and *Men, Women and the Mystery of Love: Practical Insights from John Paul II's Love and Responsibility.*